HOUGHTON MIFFLIN HARCOURT
Texas
JOURNEYS

Program Authors

James F. Baumann · David J. Chard · Jamal Cooks
J. David Cooper · Russell Gersten · Marjorie Lipson
Lesley Mandel Morrow · John J. Pikulski · Héctor H. Rivera
Mabel Rivera · Shane Templeton · Sheila W. Valencia
Catherine Valentino · MaryEllen Vogt

Consulting Author
Irene Fountas

HOUGHTON MIFFLIN HARCOURT
School Publishers

Welcome, Reader!

This year you will read many wonderful stories. In this first book, you will meet lots of pals, a special grandpa, and a curious monkey who gets into trouble. You will read about neighborhood helpers and a cat who takes a ride on a train. Your reading will get stronger each day!

Are you ready to begin your reading journey? Just turn the page!

Sincerely,

The Authors

Around the Neighborhood

Big Idea Everyone can be a good neighbor.

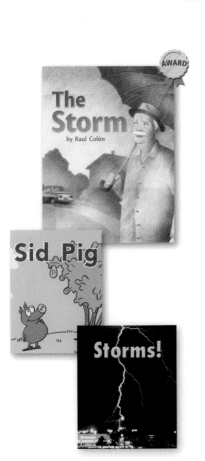

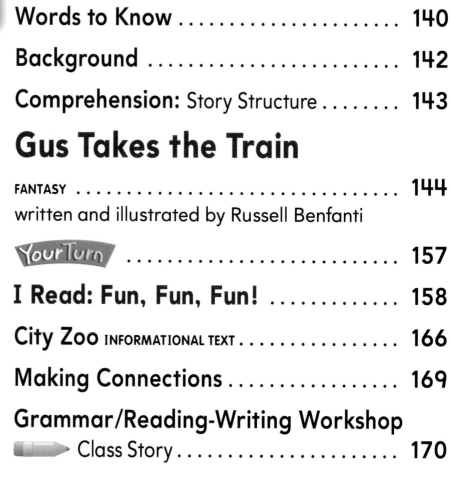

Around the Neighborhood

Unit 1

Big Idea

Everyone can be
a good neighbor.

Selections

9

✔ **WORDS TO KNOW**
HIGH-FREQUENCY WORDS

**play
be
and
help
with
you**

Vocabulary Reader

Context Cards

TEKS 1.3H identify/read high-frequency words; **ELPS 1F** use accessible language to learn new language; **3B** expand/internalize initial English vocabulary

Read Together

Words to Know

- Read each Context Card.

- Make up a sentence that uses a blue word.

1

play
These pals like to play in the park.

2

be
They like to be on the same team.

3 **and**

The children share the paper **and** paint.

4 **help**

These pals **help** each other wash the dog.

5 **with**

The boy was in a show **with** his pals.

6 **you**

I like when **you** play this game with me.

Background

✓ **WORDS TO KNOW** **How to Be a Good Pal**

1. First, you need to find a pal.

2. Smile and say hello.

3. Ask the pal to play.

4. Take turns with your pal.

5. Be kind.

6. Help your pal.

pet

Who Can Be a Pal?

boy

girl

mom

dad

TEKS **1.4C** establish purpose/monitor comprehension; **1.13** identify topic/explain author's purpose; **1.14A** restate main idea; **1.14B** identify important facts/details; **RC-1(A)** establish reading purposes; **ELPS 1E** internalize new basic/academic language; **4F** use visual/contextual/peer/ teacher support to read/comprehend texts

Comprehension
Read Together

 **✓ TARGET SKILL** Main Idea

Most nonfiction selections have one **topic**. The topic is the one big idea that the selection is about. The **main idea** is the most important idea about the topic. **Details** are facts that tell more about the main idea.

As you read **What Is a Pal?**, think about the topic and main idea. Tell about them in your own words. Fill in a web.

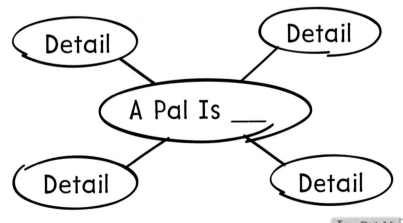

✔ **WORDS TO KNOW**

play	help
be	with
and	you

✔ **TARGET SKILL**

Main Idea Tell the important idea about a topic.

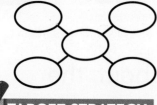

✔ **TARGET STRATEGY**

Summarize Stop to tell important ideas as you read.

GENRE

Informational text gives facts about a topic.

TEKS **1.4B** ask questions/seek clarification/ locate details about texts; **1.13** identify topic/ explain author's purpose; **1.14B** identify important facts/details; **ELPS** **4D** use prereading supports to comprehend texts

Meet the Author and Photographer

Nina Crews

Nina Crews comes from a very creative family. Her parents, Donald Crews and Ann Jonas, are both well-known artists. For her own artwork, Ms. Crews likes to make collages out of photos.

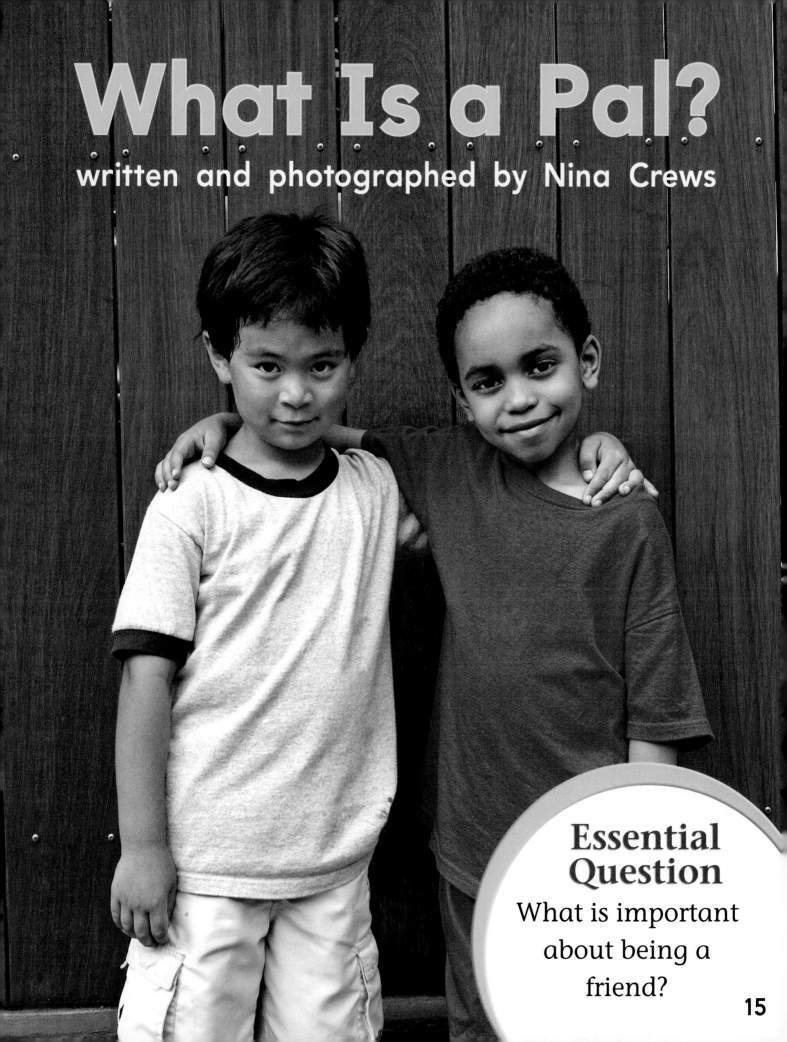

What Is a Pal?

written and photographed by Nina Crews

15

A pal can help you.

Sam and Nat can help Dan.

A pal can play with you.

Tad, Cam, and Nan can play.

A pal can be a pet.

A pal can be Dad.

A pal can be with you.

A pal is fun to be with!

Are you a pal?

Your Turn

---

1. In the story, the word <u>play</u> means —

⬭ to have fun

⬭ to help

⬭ to work

TEKS 1.6C

---

2. ✔ **TARGET SKILL** **Main Idea**

Why is it fun to be with a pal? **TEKS** 1.4B, 1.14A, 1.14B, 1.24C; **ELPS** 4K

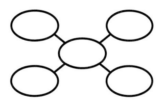

3. Oral Language Tell a partner two things you learned about being a pal. Speak clearly. Use the Retelling Cards. **TEKS** 1.14B, 1.28

Retelling Cards

TEKS **1.4B** ask questions/seek clarification/locate details about texts; **1.6C** use syntax/context to determine meaning; **1.14A** restate main idea; **1.14B** identify important facts/details; **1.24C** record information in visual formats; **1.28** share information/ideas by speaking clearly; **ELPS** **4K** employ analytical skills to demonstrate comprehension

Nan
and
Dan

✔ **PHONICS SKILL**

Short **a**
Consonants **p, f**

✔ **WORDS TO KNOW**

and
help
with

 TEKS 1.3A(i) decode words with consonants;
1.3A(ii) decode words with vowels; 1.3H
identify/read high-frequency words

Nan
and
Dan

by Donald Busch
illustrated by Rick Powell

Nan can tap a pan.

Nan can help Dan tap.

Dan can tap and tap!

Nan can pat a cat.

Dan can pat a cat.

The fat cat can nap.

Dan can nap with Nan.

Friends Forever

Connect to Poetry

✔ **WORDS TO KNOW**

play	help
be	with
and	you

GENRE

Poetry uses the sounds of words to show pictures and feelings.

TEXT FOCUS

Rhyme is words with the same ending sound, like <u>blue</u> and <u>two</u>. Clap when you hear words that rhyme at the end of lines.

 TEKS **1.3H** identify/read high-frequency words; **1.8** respond to/use rhythm/rhyme/alliteration; **ELPS 4G** demonstrate comprehension through shared reading/retelling/responding/note-taking

Friends Forever

How can **you** **be** a good friend?
You can **play** **with** your friends.
You can share with friends **and**
help them.

Damon & Blue

Damon & Blue
Just us two
Cruising up the avenue.

You strut, you glide
But mark our stride
Can't beat us when we're
   side by side.

by Nikki Grimes

Wait for Me

Wait for me
and I'll be there
and we'll walk home together,
if it's raining
puddle pails
or if it's sunny weather.

Wait for me
and I'll be there
and we'll walk home together.
You wear red
and I'll wear blue,
and we'll be friends forever.

by Sarah Wilson

Jambo

Jambo Jambo
ambo ambo
mbo mbo
bo bo bo
o o o
bo bo bo
mbo mbo
ambo ambo
Jambo Jambo
HI! HELLO!
Did you Did you
did you know
Jambo means
hello hello!

*by Sundaira
Morninghouse*

Respond to Poetry

- Listen to the poems again. Join in!
- Say more rhyming lines that could be added to one of the poems. **TEKS** 1.8

Making Connections

Read Together

 Text to Self　　　　**TEKS** 1.19A, RC-1(F)

Write Sentences Write sentences to tell your classmates about favorite things you do with your pals.

 Text to Text　　　　**TEKS** 1.4B, 1.14B, RC-1(F)

Discuss Characters How are the friends in the poems like the pals in the story **What Is a Pal?**

 Text to World　　　　**TEKS** RC-1(F)

Connect to Social Studies Can neighbors be pals? What are some things that good neighbors do?

 TEKS 1.4B ask questions/seek clarification/locate details about texts; **1.14B** identify important facts/details; **1.19A** write brief compositions; **RC-1(F)** make connections to experiences/texts/community; **ELPS 1E** internalize new basic/academic language; **3G** express opinions/ideas/feelings

37

TEKS **1.6A** identify nouns/verbs; **1.20A(ii)** understand/use nouns; **ELPS** **1E** internalize new basic/academic language; **5E** employ increasingly complex grammatical structures

Grammar

Nouns Some words name people. Some words name animals. Words that name people and animals are called **nouns**.

Nouns for People

boy

dad

sister

baby

Nouns for Animals

dog

cat

pig

cow

Talk about each picture with a partner. Name the nouns you see. Then write a noun from the box to name each picture. Use another sheet of paper.

| man | bird | girl | fish | mom |

1.

2.

3.

4.

5.

Grammar in Writing

Share your writing with a partner. Talk about the nouns you used.

Writing About Us

Read Together

✓**Ideas** Dan drew and wrote about his pals. Then he thought about what details to add. He added a picture of a ball and a **label**.

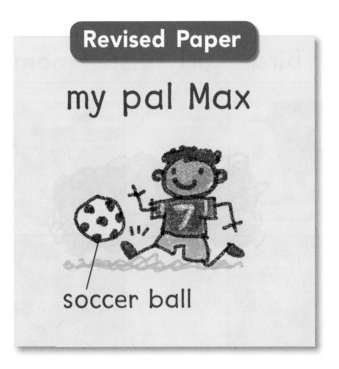

Revised Paper

my pal Max

soccer ball

Writing Traits Checklist

✓**Ideas** Does my paper have interesting details about my pals?

✓ Did I use nouns in my labels?

✓ Did I write letters neatly and correctly?

40

What do the details in Dan's paper tell you about his pals? Now revise your own writing. Use the Checklist.

Final Paper

My Pals

my mom

van

my brother

computer

my pal Max

soccer ball

Star

rabbit

2

WORKS TO KNOW
HIGH-FREQUENCY WORDS

he

look

have

for

too

what

Vocabulary Reader

Context Cards

 TEKS 1.3H identify/read high-frequency words; **ELPS 1F** use accessible language to learn new language; **3B** expand/internalize initial English vocabulary

Words to Know

- Read each Context Card.

- Choose two blue words. Use them in sentences.

1

he

He walked across the street with his friends.

2

look

Children look at water from the fire hose.

3 have

Firefighters have fast trucks to get to a fire.

4 for

The girl went to the doctor for a visit.

5 too

They took hats and the sunblock, too.

6 what

What do people do to help you feel safe?

Background

✔ **WORDS TO KNOW** **Storm Clouds**

1. Look at the sky!

2. What does the boy see?

3. Dark clouds have moved closer.

4. There is thunder, too.

5. The boy heads for home.

6. He wants to stay dry!

How do you know a storm is coming?
What do you see and hear in a storm?

44

TEKS 1.4C establish purpose/monitor comprehension; **1.9B** describe/analyze characters; **RC–1(A)** establish reading purposes; **RC–1(D)** make inferences/use textual evidence; **ELPS 1E** internalize new basic/academic language; **4F** use visual/contextual/peer/teacher support to read/comprehend texts

Comprehension

Read Together

✓ **TARGET SKILL** Understanding Characters

Characters are the people and animals in a story. When you read, think about what the characters say and do. Good readers use these clues to figure out how characters feel and why they do the things they do.

Read **The Storm**. Use the words and pictures to figure out what Pop says and does to help Tim.

Speaking	Acting

The Storm
by Raúl Colón

✔ WORDS TO KNOW

he	for
look	too
have	what

✔ TARGET SKILL

Understanding Characters Tell more about the characters.

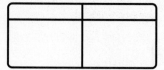

✔ TARGET STRATEGY

Infer/Predict Use clues to figure out more about story parts.

GENRE

Realistic fiction is a made-up story that could happen in real life.

TEKS **1.4C** establish purpose/monitor comprehension; **1.9B** describe/analyze characters; **RC-1(D)** make inferences/use textual evidence; **ELPS 4J** employ inferential skills to demonstrate comprehension

Meet the Author and Illustrator

Raúl Colón

As a little boy in Puerto Rico, Raúl Colón was often very sick. He spent a lot of time inside, drawing. He even made his own comic books. Today Mr. Colón lives in New York and works as an artist and a writer.

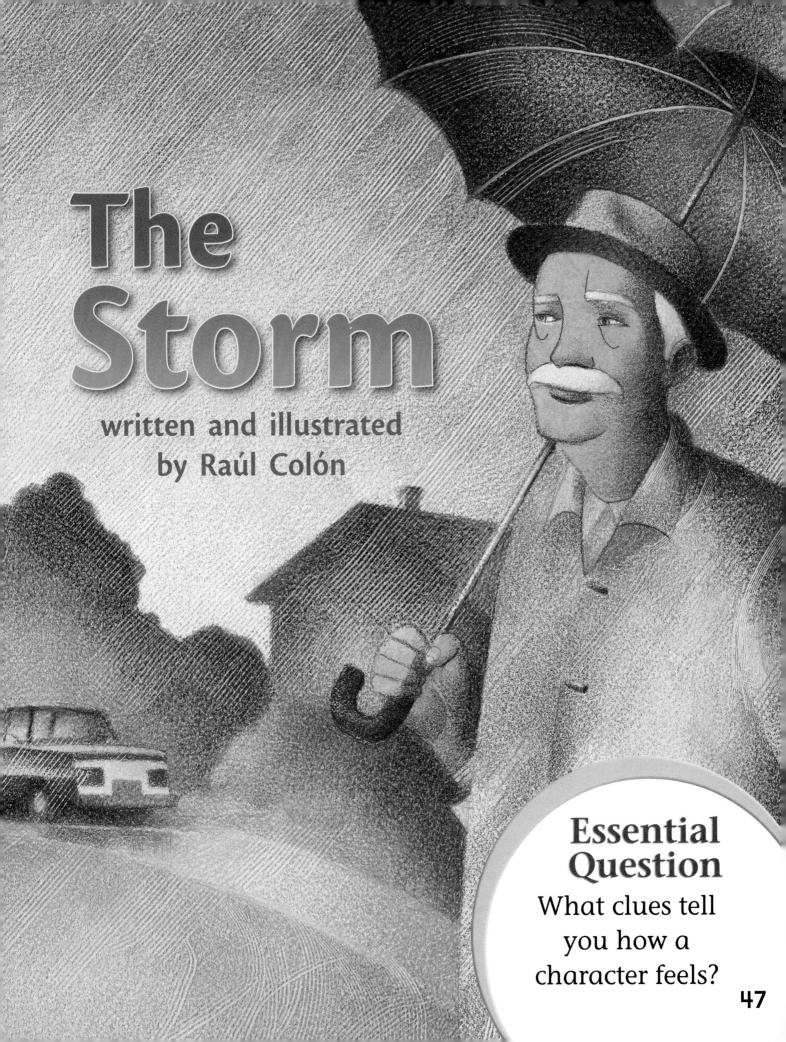

The Storm

written and illustrated
by Raúl Colón

Essential Question

What clues tell you how a character feels?

Pop has come in.
Look! He is wet.

Tim and Rip ran to him.

Tim, Rip, and Pop have fun.

Tim had to go to bed.

What did Tim and Rip see?

Tim hid in his bed!
Rip hid, too!

53

Look what Pop had for Tim.
Tim had a sip.

Pop had a hug for Tim.
He had a hug for Rip, too.

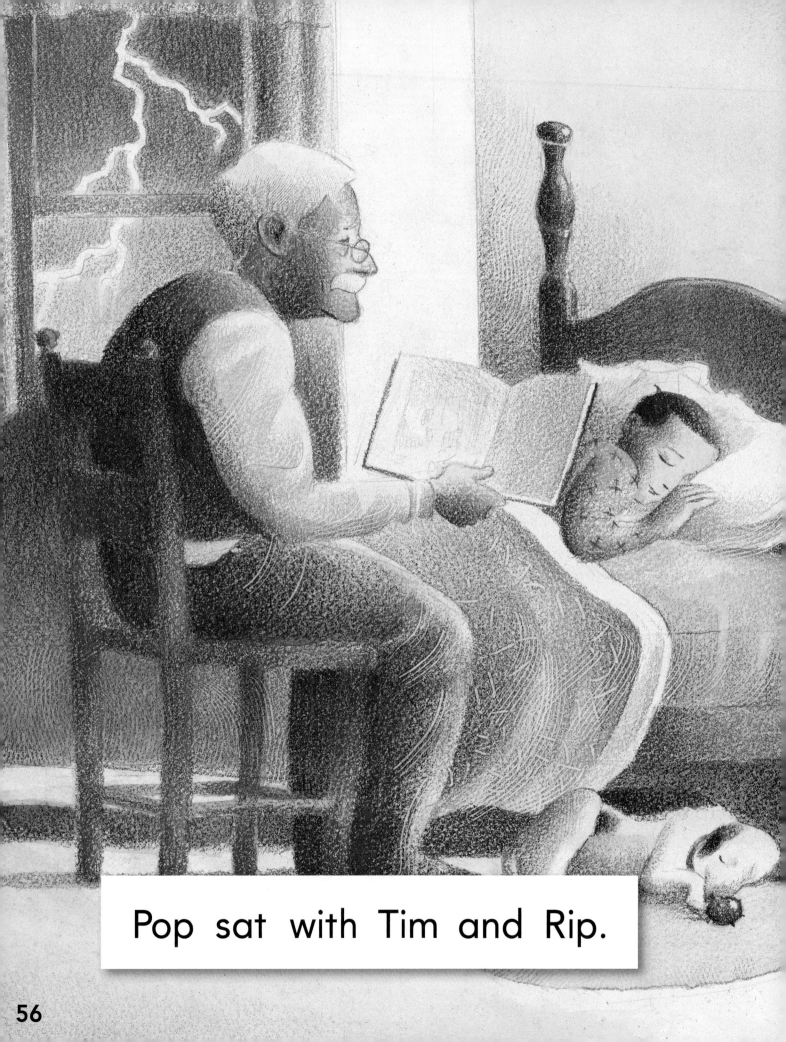

Pop sat with Tim and Rip.

1. What does Pop do to help when Tim is scared?

- ⬭ Pop sends Tim to bed.
- ⬭ Pop gives Tim a hug.
- ⬭ Pop plays ball with Tim.

TEKS 1.9A

2. ✓ **TARGET SKILL** **Understanding Characters**
Look at page 55. What does Pop do? Why? TEKS 1.4B, 1.9B, RC-1(D); ELPS 4J

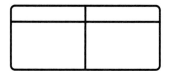

3. Oral Language Take turns with a partner. Tell what happened in the story. Use the Retelling Cards to tell the events in order.
TEKS 1.9A, RC-1(E)

Retelling Cards

TEKS **1.4B** ask questions/seek clarification/locate details about texts; **1.9A** retell story events; **1.9B** describe/analyze characters; **RC-1(D)** make inferences/use textual evidence; **RC-1(E)** retell/act out important story events; **ELPS 4J** employ inferential skills to demonstrate comprehension

Sid Pig

Sid Pig

by Damian Byrne
illustrated by Ethan Long

58

Look at Sid Pig.
He can see a fig.

It is a big fig.
It is fat, too!

Can Sid tap the fig?

Can Sid tip the fig?
Can Sid hit the fig?

Sid Pig did it!
Sid can have his fig.

Sid bit his big fat fig.
Mmm!   Mmm!

Connect to Science

GENRE

Informational text gives facts on a topic. Find storm facts during shared reading. This is from a science textbook.

TEXT FOCUS

Photographs show true pictures with important details. Use these photographs to find out information about storms.

 TEKS **1.3H** identify/read high-frequency words; **1.4B** ask questions/seek clarification/ locate details about texts; **1.4C** establish purpose/monitor comprehension; **1.24A** gather evidence

Storms!

A storm is a strong wind with rain or snow. It may have hail or sleet. Warm, light air goes up quickly. It mixes with high, cold air. Look! It's a storm.

This is a lightning storm in Pampa, Texas.

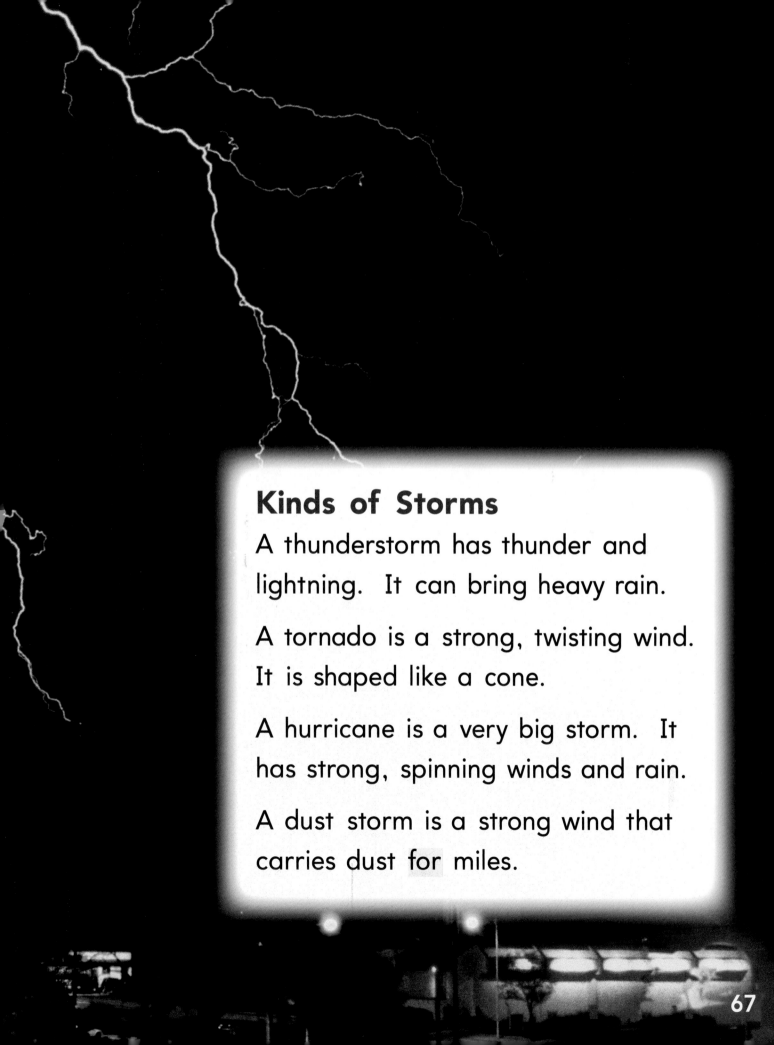

Kinds of Storms

A thunderstorm has thunder and lightning. It can bring heavy rain.

A tornado is a strong, twisting wind. It is shaped like a cone.

A hurricane is a very big storm. It has strong, spinning winds and rain.

A dust storm is a strong wind that carries dust for miles.

rain gauge

thermometer

wind gauge

wind sock

Measuring Storms

A scientist has tools for measuring storms. He measures heat and cold. He measures the wind. He measures rainfall and snowfall, too.

What storms have you seen?

Making Connections

The Storm
by Raúl Colón

Storms!

Read Together

 Text to Self — TEKS 1.19A, RC-1(F)

Write Sentences Write about a storm you saw. How did the weather change?

 Text to Text — TEKS 1.4B, 1.29, RC-1(F)

Retell and Describe With a small group, talk about storms you have learned about. Describe the kind of storm Tim and Rip saw. Listen to each other. Then work together to share what your group said.

 Text to World — TEKS RC-1(F)

Connect to Social Studies How can neighbors in a community help each other during a storm? Draw a picture.

 TEKS **1.4B** ask questions/seek clarification/locate details about texts; **1.19A** write brief compositions; **1.29** follow discussion rules; **RC-1(F)** make connections to experiences/texts/community; **ELPS** **1E** internalize new basic/academic language; **2I** demonstrate listening comprehension of spoken English; **3D** speak using content-area vocabulary; **3E** share information in cooperative learning interactions

Grammar

Nouns Some words name places. Some words name things. Words that name places and things are called **nouns**.

Nouns for Places

- house
- sky
- road
- garden
- pond

Nouns for Things

- book
- chair
- bed
- door
- rug

Turn and Talk

Talk about each picture with a partner. Name the nouns you see. Then write a noun from the box to name each picture. Use another sheet of paper.

| milk   coat   room   city   clock |

1.

4.

2.

5.

3.

Grammar in Writing

Share your writing. Talk about the nouns you used.

Writing About Us

☑ **Ideas** Kit drew and wrote about her family trip to the beach. Then she thought of new details. She added a **caption** to explain her picture.

Revised Paper

We saw a fish.

Writing Traits Checklist

☑ **Ideas** Does my paper have interesting details about my family trip?

☑ Do my captions explain the pictures?

☑ Did I use nouns to name places or things?

Look for nouns in Kit's final paper. Then revise your own writing. Use the Checklist.

Final Paper

Our Trip to the Beach

my family

a castle we made

We saw a fish.

We found shells.

Curious George at School
based on Margret and H. A. Rey's Curious George

Max Fox and Lon Ox

School Long Ago

✓ **WORDS TO KNOW**
HIGH-FREQUENCY WORDS

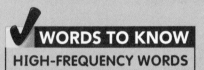

sing
do
they
find
funny
no

Vocabulary Reader

School

Context Cards

 TEKS 1.3H identify/read high-frequency words; **ELPS** 1F use accessible language to learn new language; 3B expand/internalize initial English vocabulary

Words to Know

Read Together

● Read each Context Card.

● Ask a question that uses one of the blue words.

1 sing

These children sing with the music teacher.

2 do

The school principal has many things to do.

3 they

They like to work together in class.

4 find

The librarian helps children find books.

5 funny

The art teacher drew a funny animal.

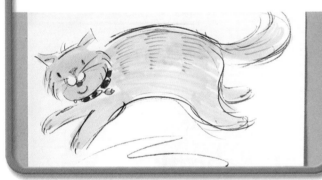

6 no

It is safe to cross when no cars are coming.

TEKS **1.3H** identify/read high-frequency words; **1.6D** categorize words; **ELPS** **4D** use prereading supports to comprehend texts; **4F** use visual/contextual/peer/teacher support to read/comprehend texts

Background

✔ WORDS TO KNOW One School Day

1. Children do a lot at school.

2. They read books.

3. They find out many things!

4. They sing songs.

5. They draw funny pictures.

6. Are they done?
   No, they do lots more!

art materials

Things To Do at School

read books

eat lunch

learn math

sing songs

TEKS 1.4C establish purpose/monitor comprehension; **RC–1(A)** establish reading purposes; **ELPS 1E** internalize new basic/academic language; **4F** use visual/contextual/peer/teacher support to read/comprehend texts

Comprehension

✓ **TARGET SKILL** Sequence of Events

Many stories tell about events in the order in which they happen. This order is called the **sequence of events.** The sequence of events is what happens **first**, **next**, and **last** in a story.

| First | Next | Last |

As you read **Curious George at School**, think about what happens first, next, and last.

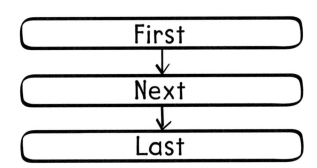

First

↓

Next

↓

Last

JOURNEYS DIGITAL **Powered by** DESTINATIONReading®
Comprehension Activities: Lesson 3

Curious George at School
based on Margret and H. A. Rey's
Curious George

✔ **WORDS TO KNOW**

sing	find
do	funny
they	no

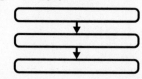

✔ **TARGET SKILL**

Sequence of Events
Tell the order in which
things happen.

✔ **TARGET STRATEGY**

Monitor/Clarify If
a part doesn't make
sense, read it again.

GENRE

A **fantasy** is a story
that could not happen
in real life.

TEKS **1.4C** establish purpose/monitor
comprehension; **1.9A** retell story events;
RC-1(C) monitor/adjust comprehension;
ELPS 4D use prereading supports to comprehend texts

Meet the Creators

Margret and H. A. Rey

Children all over the world
love Curious George! The Reys'
books have been published in
Spanish, French, Swedish,
Japanese, and many other
languages. Since the Reys
wrote their first book about
the curious little monkey,
George has starred in more
than 40 books, a TV show,
and a movie.

Curious George at School

based on Margret and H. A. Rey's
Curious George

Essential Question

Why is the order of story events important?

This is George.
He can help a lot.

George can sing.
He is funny.

He can see the paints.

Mix, mix, mix a bit.
Mix, mix, mix a lot!

It is a big mess!

George ran.
What did he find?

He got a mop.
He had a big job to do.

No, no!
It is a big, BIG mess!
George is sad, sad, sad.

Kids help him do a big job.
They can help him a lot.
He is not sad!

1. In the story, the word <u>find</u> means —

⬭ to lose

⬭ to hide

⬭ to discover

TEKS 1.6C

2. ✔ TARGET SKILL **Sequence of Events**

Retell the important events that happen in the beginning, middle, and end of the story.

TEKS 1.9A, RC-1(E); **ELPS** 4G

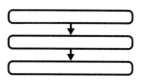

3. Oral Language Work with a partner. Use the Retelling Cards to tell your favorite part of the story. **TEKS** 1.9A

Retelling Cards

 TEKS 1.6C use syntax/context to determine meaning; **1.9A** retell story events; **RC-1(E)** retell/act out important story events; **ELPS** 4G demonstrate comprehension through shared reading/retelling/responding/note-taking

89

✔ **PHONICS SKILL**

Short **o**
Inflection **-s**
Consonants **l, x**

✔ **WORDS TO KNOW**

sing
do
no

TEKS **1.3A(i)** decode words with consonants;
1.3A(ii) decode words with vowels; **1.3E** read
words with inflectional endings; **1.3H** identify/
read high-frequency words; **ELPS** **4A** learn English
sound-letter relationships/decode

Max Fox and Lon Ox

by David McCoy
illustrated by Kristin Sorra

Max Fox is six.

Lon Ox is not six.
Sad Lon sits and sits.

Max got a big box.
It is a big, big box!

What is in it?
It is a sax!

Max plays. Bip, bop!
Bip, bop, bop, bop!

Can Lon Ox play? No!
What can Lon Ox do?

Lon Ox can sing!

Connect to Social Studies

✔ **WORDS TO KNOW**

sing	find
do	funny
they	no

GENRE

Informational text gives facts about a topic. This is from a social studies textbook. Read to find out what the topic is.

TEXT FOCUS

A **chart** is a drawing that lists information in a clear way. What can you learn from the chart on page 100?

 TEKS **1.3H** identify/read high-frequency words; **1.13** identify topic/explain author's purpose; **1.14D** use text features to locate information; **ELPS** **4F** use visual/contextual/peer/teacher support to read/comprehend texts

School Long Ago

How did children get to school? Was going to school long ago different from going to school today? Let's find out! There were no school buses long ago. Some children had to walk far to get to school.

What did children bring to school?
Long ago, children did not have
backpacks. They carried their
things for school in their arms.
Children did not have a lot
of paper long ago. They
used chalk to write on small
boards called slates.

What did children learn?

Long ago, children learned reading, writing, and math. Some teachers taught children funny songs to sing. What do children learn in school today?

Then	Now

Making Connections

Read Together

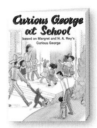

 Text to Self   **TEKS** 1.7A, RC-1(F)

Connect to Experiences Think of something Curious George did that you have also done. Write about it.

 Text to Text   **TEKS** 1.10, RC-1(F)

Compare Stories Is the story about Curious George true or make-believe? How do you know? Tell how you know **School Long Ago** is a true story.

 Text to World   **TEKS** 1.24C, RC-1(F)

Draw a Map Draw a map of your classroom. Show where you sit.

 TEKS 1.7A connect stories/fables to personal experiences; **1.10** distinguish true stories from fantasies; **1.24C** record information in visual formats; **RC-1(F)** make connections to experiences/texts/community; **ELPS 3E** share information in cooperative learning interactions

TEKS **1.6A** identify nouns/verbs; **1.20A(i)** understand/use verbs; **ELPS** **1E** internalize new basic/academic language; **5E** employ increasingly complex grammatical structures in writing

Grammar

Read Together

Action Verbs Some words tell what people and animals do. These action words are called **verbs**.

hop

play

jog

hit

Turn and Talk

Write a verb from the box to name the action in each picture. Use another sheet of paper. Then act out one of the verbs. Have a partner guess the verb.

paint   help   sip   mix

1.

2.

3.

4.

Grammar in Writing

When you revise your writing, use action verbs to tell about things you do. Turn to a partner and identify the words that name actions in your writing.

Writing About Us

✓ **Word Choice** Writers use exact nouns to help give readers a clear picture.

Leah wrote about school activities. Later, she changed **things** to a noun that is exact.

Revised Draft

                    books
We all read ~~things~~.
                  ^

Writing Traits Checklist

✓ **Word Choice** Did I use nouns that are exact?

✓ Did I use action verbs to tell about things I do?

✓ Did I write letters neatly and correctly?

104

Find nouns and verbs in Leah's final copy.
Then revise your writing. Use the Checklist.

Final Paper

Fun at School

We all read books.

I write stories.

Ani feeds our mice.

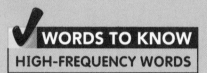

✓ **WORDS TO KNOW**

HIGH-FREQUENCY WORDS

my

here

who

all

does

me

Vocabulary
Reader

Context
Cards

TEKS 1.3H identify/read high-frequency words; **ELPS** 1F use accessible language to learn new language; 3B expand/internalize initial English vocabulary

Words to Know

Read Together

- **Read each** Context Card.

- **Tell about a picture, using the blue word.**

1

my

The dentist will check my teeth.

2

here

The firefighters keep their trucks here.

3 who

Who brings the mail to your house?

4 all

The baker made all of these rolls.

5 does

Does this vet take care of dogs?

6 me

The zookeeper let me pet the koala.

TEKS **1.3H** identify/read high-frequency words; **RC-1(F)** make connections to experiences/texts/community; **ELPS 4D** use prereading supports to comprehend texts; **4F** use visual/contextual/peer/teacher support to read/comprehend texts

Background

Read Together

✔ **WORDS TO KNOW** **Good Neighbors**

1. Come to my neighborhood!

2. People are friendly here.

3. We all help each other.

4. How does my neighbor help?

5. She helps me plant the garden.

6. Who will I help today?

How has someone helped you?

How can you help someone?

TEKS 1.4C establish purpose/monitor comprehension; **1.14D** use text features to locate information; **RC-1(A)** establish reading purposes; **RC-1(D)** make inferences/use textual evidence; **ELPS 1E** internalize new basic/academic language; **4F** use visual/contextual/peer/teacher support to read/comprehend texts

Comprehension

Read Together

✔ **TARGET SKILL** Text and Graphic Features

Authors may use **special features** to tell about the topic of a selection. Labels and captions give information about photos. Photos, graphs, maps, and drawings help explain a topic. Good readers think about special features to understand what the author wants them to know.

As you read **Lucia's Neighborhood**, think about the special features. Use a chart like this one to tell what the author wants you to know.

Feature	Purpose

JOURNEYS DIGITAL Powered by DESTINATION Reading®
Comprehension Activities: Lesson 4

Lucia's Neighborhood
by George Ancona

✓ WORDS TO KNOW

my	all
here	does
who	me

✓ TARGET SKILL

Text and Graphic Features Tell how words go with photos.

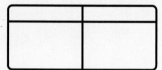

✓ TARGET STRATEGY

Question Ask questions about what you read.

GENRE

Informational text gives facts about a topic. Find facts as you read this selection.

TEKS **1.4B** ask questions/seek clarification/ locate details about texts; **1.14D** use text features to locate information; **RC-1(B)** ask literal questions of text; **ELPS 4D** use prereading supports to comprehend texts

Meet the Author and Photographer

George Ancona

What do you like to do for fun? George Ancona enjoys dancing, listening to salsa music, and spending time with his grandchildren. He does not like to watch TV or send e-mail. Mr. Ancona has written many books, including **Mi Música/My Music.**

35

Lucia's Neighborhood

written and photographed by George Ancona

Essential Question

What information do words and pictures give?

Hi! I am Lucia.
Can I get a goal?

Yes! We win.
We all get pins.

Bakery

What can Mom and I do?
Look what we get here.

I can look at pets here.
It is fun.

Mom let me get a plant here.
It is not big yet.

Who can fix the street?
Here is the man who can fix it.

Garage

Who can fix a car?
Here is the man who can fix it.

Who has on firefighter's pants? They are too big to fit me yet!

Does the librarian help me?
Yes!

We sit and look at my book.

My Home

Is it fun to be home?
You bet it is!

1. What is the main idea of the story?

◯ Lucia can get a goal.

◯ It is good to be back home.

◯ People make a neighborhood special.

TEKS 1.14A

2. ✔ **TARGET SKILL** **Text and Graphic Features**
Where do Lucia and her Mom get food?
What kind of food is it? **TEKS** 1.4B, 1.14D, 1.24C; **ELPS** 4K

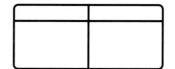

3. **Oral Language** Tell a partner two places you would like to visit in Lucia's neighborhood. Use the Retelling Cards and speak clearly.
TEKS 1.14B, 1.28

Retelling Cards

TEKS **1.4B** ask questions/seek clarification/locate details about texts; **1.14A** restate main idea; **1.14B** identify important facts/details; **1.14D** use text features to locate information; **1.24C** record information in visual formats; **1.28** share information/ideas by speaking clearly; **ELPS** **4K** employ analytical skills to demonstrate comprehension

Ken and Vic
by Kate Pistone
Illustrated by Deborah Melmon

✔ **PHONICS SKILL**

Short **e**
Consonants **j, k, v**

✔ **WORDS TO KNOW**

here
does

TEKS 1.3A(i) decode words with consonants; 1.3A(ii) decode words with vowels; 1.3H identify/read high-frequency words; **ELPS 4A** learn English sound-letter relationships/decode; **4B** recognize directionality of English reading

Ken and Vic

by Kate Pistone

illustrated by Deborah Melmon

Here is Ken.
Here is Vic.

Ken has tan bags.
Vic has bags with dots.

Ken gets his bat.
It is in his bag.

Does Ken get a hit?
Yes! It is a big hit!
Top job, Ken!

Can Vic get it?
Yes! Vic tags Ken!
Top job, Vic!

Ken gets his bag.
Vic gets his bag.

Ken has a big sip.
Vic has a big sip, too.

Connect to Traditional Tales

✔ **WORDS TO KNOW**

my	all
here	does
who	me

GENRE

A **fable** is a short story in which a character learns a lesson.

TEXT FOCUS

Many tales begin with **Once upon a time.** Why do you think the storyteller uses these words?

TEKS **1.3H** identify/read high-frequency words; **1.7A** connect stories/fables to personal experiences; **1.7B** understand recurring phrases in traditional tales; **ELPS 1H** develop/expand learning strategies

City Mouse and Country Mouse

retold by Debbie O'Brien

Cast

 Country Mouse

 City Mouse

 Cat

 Once upon a time, there were two mice.

 I love my country home. Come eat with me.

 I like city food better.

Come with me to the city. We will eat like kings.

 I will come.

 Here is my home.

 Look at all this yummy food!

Meow, meow. I will have mice for lunch!

 Who is that?

 It's Cat! Run and hide.

 City Mouse, my home does not have fine food, but it is safe. I'm going back to the country.

Making Connections

 Text to Self
TEKS 1.7A, 1.19A, RC-1(F)

Respond to the Story What lesson does Country Mouse learn? Has anything like this ever happened to you? Write about it.

 Text to Text
TEKS 1.4B, 1.9B, RC-1(D), RC-1(F)

Connect to Social Studies How do Lucia and the mice feel about their neighbors? How do you know?

 Text to World
TEKS RC-1(F)

Discuss Neighborhoods Who or what makes your neighborhood special? Discuss your feelings with a partner.

TEKS 1.4B ask questions/seek clarification/locate details about texts; 1.7A connect stories/fables to personal experiences; 1.9B describe/analyze characters; 1.19A write brief compositions; RC-1(D) make inferences/use textual evidence; RC-1(F) make connections to experiences/texts/community; **ELPS** 1E internalize new basic/academic language; 3G express opinions/ideas/feelings

TEKS **1.6D** categorize words; **1.17D** edit drafts; **1.20A(iii)** understand/use adjectives; **ELPS** **5D** edit writing for standard grammar/usage; **5E** employ increasingly complex grammatical structures in writing; **5G** narrate/describe/explain in writing

Grammar

Adjectives Some words describe people, animals, places, or things. These describing words are called **adjectives**. Adjectives can describe by telling size or shape.

Adjectives for Size

tall

long

short

tiny

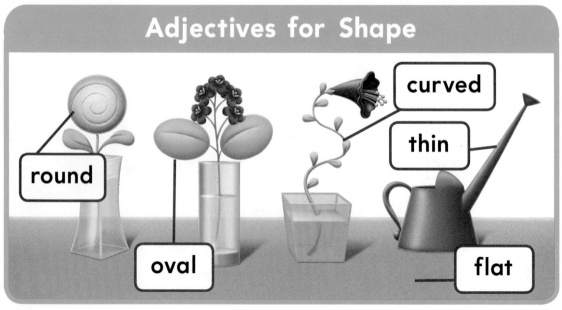

Adjectives for Shape

round

oval

curved

thin

flat

Try This!

Think of an adjective for size or shape to describe each picture. Write the word on another sheet of paper.

1.

2.

3.

4.

5.

Grammar in Writing

When you revise your class story, look for places where you can add some adjectives.

Reading-Writing Workshop: Prewrite

Writing About Us

Read Together

✔ **Word Choice** When you write a **class story**, choose interesting words that are just right! Don't use the same word again and again.

Ms. Soto's class wrote about their town. Later, they changed **big** to a clearer word.

Revised Draft

Our town has a big parade.

Funny clowns wear ~~big~~ hats.
                    tall
                      ^

Revising Checklist

✔ Does our story have interesting details?

✔ Did we use nouns that are exact?

✔ Did I write the correct verb to go with each noun?

138

Find words in Ms. Soto's class story that help you picture the parade. Then revise your class story. Use the Checklist.

Final Copy

Our Town Parade

Our town has a big parade.

Funny clowns wear tall hats.

A fire truck blasts its

horn. Horses prance

down wide streets.

Lesson 5

 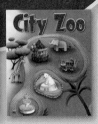 

✓ **WORDS TO KNOW**
HIGH-FREQUENCY WORDS

many
friend
full
pull
hold
good

Vocabulary Reader

Context Cards

 TEKS 1.3H identify/read high-frequency words; **ELPS** 1F use accessible language to learn new language; **3B** expand/internalize initial English vocabulary

140

Words to Know

Read Together

● Read each Context Card.

● Use a blue word to tell about something you did.

1 **many**
There are many cars on the street.

2 **friend**
She likes to ride the bus with her friend.

3 full

This train is always full of people.

4 pull

He can pull his pet in the wagon.

5 hold

She can hold up her hand to get a taxi.

6 good

The ferry is a good way to see the city.

Background

✔ **WORDS TO KNOW** **All Aboard!**

1. **Many** people like train rides.

2. It is fun to sit with a **friend**.

3. There is a shelf to **hold** your bag.

4. Sometimes all the seats are **full**.

5. Everyone will have a **good** time!

6. The conductor will **pull** the whistle cord.

A Train Ride

train   conductor   bags   seats

TEKS 1.4B ask questions/seek clarification/locate details about texts; **1.4C** establish purpose/monitor comprehension; **1.9A** retell story events; **1.9B** describe/analyze characters; **RC–1(A)** establish reading purposes; **ELPS 1E** internalize new basic/academic language; **4F** use visual/ contextual/peer/teacher support to read/comprehend texts

Comprehension

✔ **TARGET SKILL** Story Structure

A story has different parts. The **characters** are the people and animals in a story. The **setting** is when and where a story takes place. The **plot** is the order of story events. It tells what problem the characters have and how they solve it.

As you read **Gus Takes the Train**, use a story map to describe who is in the story, where they are, and what they do.

Characters	Setting
Plot	

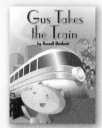

Gus Takes the Train
by Russell Benfanti

✔ WORDS TO KNOW

many	pull
friend	hold
full	good

✔ TARGET SKILL

Story Structure Tell the setting, characters, and events in a story.

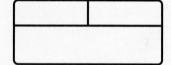

✔ TARGET STRATEGY

Analyze/Evaluate Tell how you feel about the text, and why.

GENRE

A **fantasy** is a story that could not happen in real life.

TEKS **1.9A** retell story events; **1.9B** describe/analyze characters; **RC-1(F)** make connections to experiences/texts/ community; **ELPS 4K** employ analytical skills to demonstrate comprehension

Meet the Author and Illustrator

Russell Benfanti

If you like Russell Benfanti's colorful artwork, then visit a toy store. There you will find board games, toy packages, and computer games that Mr. Benfanti designed. "I love what I do!" he says.

Gus Takes the Train

written and illustrated by Russell Benfanti

Essential Question

How does the setting make a story interesting?

Gus has to run to get the train.
He has a big bag to pull.

Run, Gus, run!

Gus cannot pull up his bag.
The conductor can help him.

The train is full.
Gus can see many kids.

Gus sat.
His big bag can go up here.

Gus met a friend!
Peg and Gus sing and play.

Peg can hold the cups for Gus.
They are too full!

Peg and Gus have a sip.
It is good!

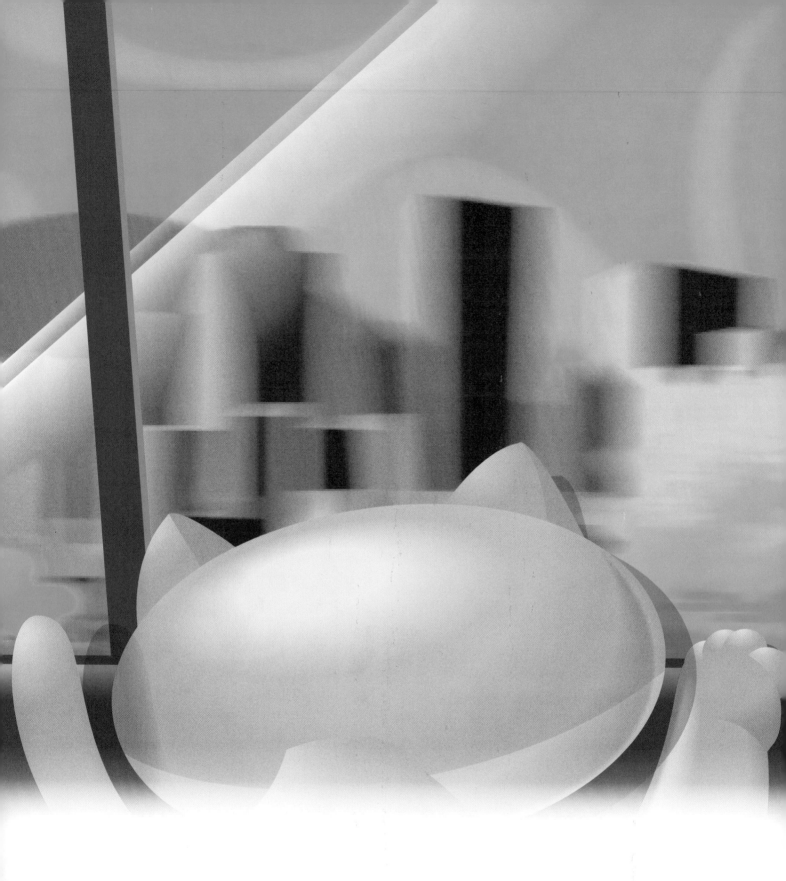

Gus can see a lot.

A funny bug is on the window!

We are here!
Gus had fun on the train.

1. In the story, the word <u>friend</u> means —

⬭ conductor

⬭ neighbor

⬭ pal

TEKS 1.6C

2. 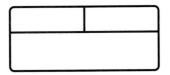 **Story Structure**

Who are the characters in the story? What do they do? Why? **TEKS** 1.9B; **ELPS** 4I

3. Oral Language Act out important events from the story with a partner. Be sure the events are in order. **TEKS** 1.9A, RC-1(E)

 TEKS **1.6C** use syntax/context to determine meaning; **1.9A** retell story events; **1.9B** describe/analyze characters; **RC-1(E)** retell/act out important story events; **ELPS 4I** employ reading skills to demonstrate comprehension

Fun, Fun, Fun!

by Harriet Smith

Mom will hold Kim.
It is fun, fun, fun!

Bud and Jim zig.
Bud and Jim zag.

Zig, zag! Zig, zag!
It is fun, fun, fun!

Liz and Jen run.
It is fun, fun, fun!

Deb and Gus play tag.
It is fun, fun, fun!

Ted can play with Dad.
It is fun, fun, fun!

Do not quit! Have fun!
Have fun, fun, fun!

Connect to Social Studies

many	pull
friend	hold
full	good

GENRE

Informational text gives facts about a topic. What is the topic of the selection?

TEXT FOCUS

A **map** is a drawing of a place. A **key** shows what pictures on the map mean. What does each picture in the key on page 167 mean?

 TEKS **1.3H** identify/read high-frequency words; **1.13** identify topic/explain author's purpose; **1.15B** explain signs/symbols; **ELPS** **4F** use visual/contextual/peer/teacher support to read/comprehend texts

City Zoo

Welcome to the City Zoo! The zoo is full of many interesting animals. See if you can find all the animals on the map.

Key

tiger

elephant

polar bear

giraffe

We hope you have a good time
at the zoo.

- Come with your family
  and a friend.

- Hold on to your ticket.

- Have some snacks.

- Pull a wagon.

- Take pictures.

Making Connections

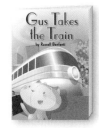

Read Together

Text to Self

TEKS 1.19A, RC-1(F)

Write a Description Write to tell your classmates about a time you went on a trip. Tell them what you saw and did.

Text to Text

TEKS 1.10, RC-1(F)

Compare Stories Think about the selections. Tell which is make-believe. Which is true? How do you know?

Text to World

TEKS RC-1(F)

Connect to Social Studies Imagine that you are traveling to study animals. Where would you go? Find that place on a map or globe.

TEKS **1.10** distinguish true stories from fantasies; **1.19A** write brief compositions; **RC-1(F)** make connections to experiences/texts/community; **ELPS 1C** use strategic learning techniques; **2E** use support to enhance/confirm understanding of spoken language

Grammar

Adjectives Some **adjectives** describe people, animals, places, or things by telling their color or how many.

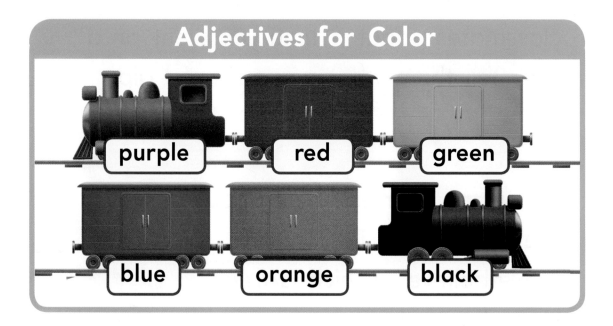

Adjectives for Color

purple red green

blue orange black

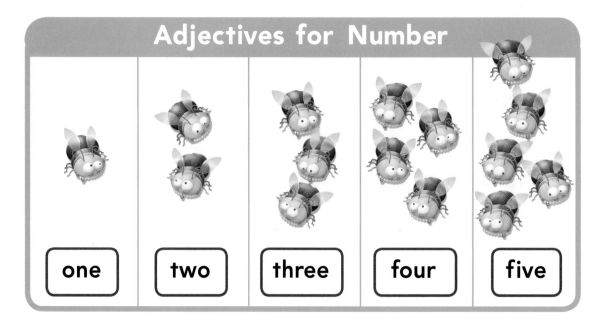

Adjectives for Number

one two three four five

Turn and Talk

Use one number adjective and one color adjective to describe each picture. Talk with your partner about how adjectives help you tell how things look.

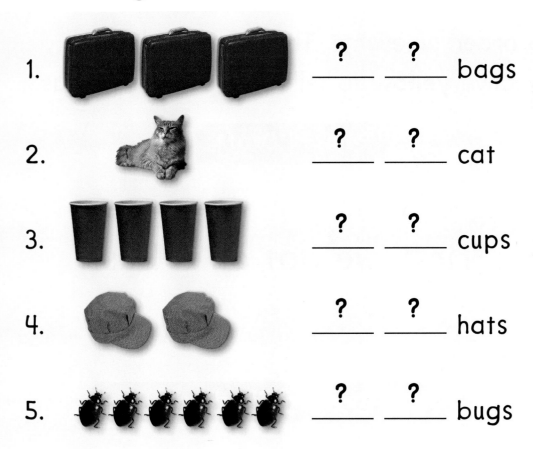

1. ? ? ____ ____ bags

2. ? ? ____ ____ cat

3. ? ? ____ ____ cups

4. ? ? ____ ____ hats

5. ? ? ____ ____ bugs

Grammar in Writing

When you revise your writing, look for places where you can add some adjectives.

Reading-Writing Workshop: Revise

Writing About Us

Read Together

✓ **Ideas** When you write a **class story**, use adjectives to describe things clearly.

Mr. Tam's class wrote about a bus trip. They used **First, Next,** and **Last** to tell the order of events. Then they added the adjective **yellow** to tell more about the bus.

Revised Draft

yellow
First, we got on a^bus.

Revising Checklist

✔ Are the story events in the correct order?

✔ Did we use words like **first, next,** and **last** to show the order?

✔ Could we tell more by adding adjectives?

172

Read the class story. Find adjectives.
Find words that tell order. Now help revise
your class story. Use the Checklist.

Final Copy

A City Bus Ride

Our class took a bus trip.

First, we got on a yellow bus.

Next, we sang two songs.

Last, we saw tall
buildings and
long trains.

Read the story. Then read each question. Choose the best answer for the question.

A Pet for Tim

My dad said, "Tim, you can get a pet."

My friends have pets I like.

Dan has Mac the dog.

Mac likes to run and play.

A dog is a fun pet.

Jed has Bev the bird.

It can sing and <u>speak</u>.

It says funny things.

Bev stays in.

Mel has Dot the cat.

All she does is stay in and nap!

I want a pet that can go out.

1 What is this story all about?

⬭ Friends and their pets

⬭ Dot the cat

⬭ Mac the dog

2 What kind of pet will Tim get?

⬭ Cat

⬭ Dog

⬭ Bird

3 What does the word <u>speak</u> mean?

⬭ Run

⬭ Play

⬭ Talk

GO ON ➤

Fun at the Zoo

Pam and Mom go to the zoo.

First, they go to see the cubs.

Next, they see the big cats play.

Last, Pam and Mom go to see the funny seals.

The man <u>chooses</u> Pam to help him.

Pam helps him with the fish.

1 Which animals did Pam see first?

- ⬭ Seals
- ⬭ Big cats
- ⬭ Cubs

2 What is this story mostly about?

- ⬭ A big cat
- ⬭ A trip to a zoo
- ⬭ A seal show

3 The word <u>chooses</u> means —

- ⬭ picks
- ⬭ hides
- ⬭ sings

STOP

POWER Practice

TEKS 1.15B explain signs/symbols

Signs

Signs use pictures, shapes, and words to tell what something is or to tell about something.

Write what these signs mean on a separate sheet of paper.

1. **SPEED LIMIT 35**

2.  CLOSED

3.  ONE WAY

4.

178

TEKS 1.21A form letters legibly

Handwriting

Read Together

Write each uppercase and lowercase letter correctly on a separate sheet of paper.

Aa Bb Cc Dd

Ee Ff Gg Hh Ii

Jj Kk Ll Mm

Nn Oo Pp Qq

Rr Ss Tt Uu Vv

Ww Xx Yy Zz

TEKS 1.23A generate topics/formulate questions

Brainstorm Research Topics

 Read Together

A research report answers a question about a topic. Brainstorm a class list of interesting topics you want to learn about. List the topics.

As you brainstorm with your classmates, be a good listener. Raise your hand to share ideas. Remember to follow your class's discussion rules.

I want to know more about kinds of planes.

TEKS **1.27A** listen attentively/ask relevant questions; **1.29** follow discussion rules

Having a Discussion

Read Together

Think about what you read in **Storms!**
Share what you learned about storms with
a few classmates.   Follow these rules.

Rules for Discussion

- Stay on topic when you speak.

- Speak clearly.

- Do not speak too fast or too slow.

- Speak in complete sentences.

As a listener, be sure to look at
the person who is talking.   Listen
carefully.   Ask questions about the
topic to help you understand the
information you hear.   Raise
your hand to talk.

18

TEKS 1.1C sequence the letters of the alphabet; 1.21A form letters legibly

Handwriting

Write each row of letters neatly on a separate sheet of paper. Fill in missing uppercase and lowercase letters.

1. A   B   C   ☐

2. F   G   ☐   I

3. p   ☐   r   s

4. ☐   x   y   z

TEKS 1.23A generate topics/formulate questions

Brainstorm Research Topics

Read Together

Get into small groups. Generate a list of topics your group would like to research. List the topics on a chart like the one below.

As you brainstorm with others, follow your class's discussion rules. Keep the list for Lesson 3.

Possible Topics to Research	Person Who Suggested Topic
1.	
2.	
3.	
4.	
5.	

TEKS **1.27A** listen attentively/ask relevant questions; **1.29** follow discussion rules

Having a Discussion

Read
Together

Think about what you read in **School Long Ago**. Share what you learned about schools with a few classmates. Follow these rules.

Rules for Discussion

- Stay on topic when you speak.

- Speak clearly.

- Do not speak too fast or too slow.

- Speak in complete sentences.

As a listener, be sure to look at the person who is talking. Listen carefully. Ask questions about the topic to help you understand the information you hear. Raise your hand to talk.

TEKS 1.1C sequence the letters of the alphabet; 1.21A form letters legibly

Handwriting

Read Together

Write each row of letters neatly on a separate sheet of paper. Fill in the missing uppercase and lowercase letters.

1. D ☐ F G

2. M N O ☐

3. r s ☐ u

4. a ☐ c d

185

TEKS 1.23A generate topics/formulate questions

Choose a Research Topic

A research report answers a question about a topic. Use your list of topics from Lesson 2 and narrow your list to one or two topics. Keep your new list for Lesson 4.

Ask yourself these questions to narrow your list:

1. Which topic do I already know about?

2. Which topic would be the most interesting to learn about?

3. Which topic has the most information available?

TEKS **1.15A** follow written multi-step directions; **1.15B** explain signs/symbols

Signs and Symbols

Read Together

Think about **Lucia's Neighborhood**. What signs did Lucia see in her neighborhood?

Write a meaning for this sign and symbol on a separate sheet of paper.

1.

2.

 **Try This!**

Draw a symbol that could stand for a school or a park. Have a partner tell you what your symbol means.

187

TEKS 1.4B ask questions/seek clarification/locate details about texts; 1.20C ask questions with subject-verb inversion

Asking Questions

When you ask a **question**, a question word or a verb often comes first. The words in the answer often change order.

Question	Where **is the mouse?**
Answer	**The mouse is** in the city.

Let's read together **City Mouse and Country Mouse** on pages 132–134. Then write questions about story details that you want to know more about, such as **Where did the cat come from?** Look back at the story and think about it to find answers to the questions.

Write the answers.

TEKS 1.27A listen attentively/ask relevant questions; 1.29 follow discussion rules

Having a Discussion

Read
Together

Think about what you read in **Lucia's Neighborhood**. Share what you learned about neighborhoods with a few classmates. Follow these rules.

Rules for Discussion

• Stay on topic when you speak.

• Speak clearly.

• Do not speak too fast or too slow.

• Speak in complete sentences.

As a listener, be sure to look at the person who is talking. Listen carefully. Ask questions about the topic to help you understand the information you hear. Raise your hand to talk.

TEKS 1.1C sequence the letters of the alphabet; 1.21A form letters legibly

Handwriting

Write each row of letters neatly on a separate sheet of paper. Fill in the missing uppercase and lowercase letters.

1. | T | U | V | |

2. | | M | N | O |

3. | g | | i | j |

4. | p | q | | s |

Put all the letters in ABC order. Write your answer on a separate sheet of paper.

TEKS 1.23A generate topics/formulate questions

Choose a Research Topic

Review your list of topics from Lesson 3. Work with a partner to select one topic. Keep these questions in mind:

1. Which topic do I already know about?

2. Which topic would be the most interesting to learn about?

3. Which topic has the most information available?

Write your final topic on a separate sheet of paper. Then begin thinking of questions you have about your topic. Keep your topic to use in Lesson 5.

TEKS 1.17E publish/share writing

Publishing  Read Together

Share your class story by making a big book. Use teamwork to make the big book. Make sure each person has a job. Follow discussion rules as you work.

- Copy one sentence on each page.

- Draw big pictures.

- Make a cover.

TEKS **1.6E** alphabetize/use dictionary; **1.21A** form letters legibly

ABC Order

Write these words on another sheet of paper.

> dog   yellow   mouse   sand

Underline the first letter of each word. Use the first letter to write the words in ABC order.

> train   table   toad   tiptoe

These words all begin with **t**. To write them in ABC order, look at the next letter. Underline the second letter in each word. Then write the words neatly in ABC order.

TEKS 1.23A generate topics/formulate questions

Ask Questions

Read Together

On another sheet of paper, make a list of questions about the research topic you chose in Lesson 4.

This list may help you get started.

Where can you find _____?

How does _____ work?

What are the good things about _____?

Read your questions to a partner.

Words to Know

Unit 1 High-Frequency Words

❶ What Is a Pal?

play
be
and
help
with
you

❹ Lucia's Neighborhood

my
here
who
all
does
me

❷ The Storm

he
look
have
for
too
what

❺ Gus Takes the Train

many
friend
full
pull
hold
good

❸ Curious George at School

sing
do
they
find
no
funny

Glossary

B

bed

A **bed** is a kind of furniture for sleeping. I sleep in my **bed**.

book

A **book** is a group of pages with words on them. **Frog and Toad** is my favorite **book**.

C

car

A **car** is a machine with four wheels. We go in a **car** to visit my grandparents.

come

To **come** means to move toward something. Maria called the puppy to **come** to her.

conductor

The **conductor** is the person in charge of a train. The train **conductor** watched the tracks closely.

curious

To be **curious** is to want to learn. Alan was **curious** about dinosaurs.

F

firefighter's

A **firefighter** is someone who puts out fires. A **firefighter's** job can be dangerous.

fun

To have **fun** is to have a good time. The children had **fun** playing tag.

G

George
George is a boy's name. My dad's name is **George**.

goal
A **goal** is a score in a game. Anita kicked the ball and made a **goal**.

H

hi
The word **hi** means hello. I say **hi** when I see someone I know.

home
A **home** is a place where people or animals live. There are six people living in my **home**.

J

job
A **job** is work for people to do. Uncle Ned has a **job** in a store.

K

kids

Kid is another word for child. My uncle tells funny stories about when he and my dad were **kids**.

L

librarian

A **librarian** works in a place where many books are kept. The **librarian** helped me find the book I was looking for.

Lucia

Lucia is a girl's name. My sister's name is **Lucia**.

M

mess

A **mess** is something that is not neat. My sister's room is a **mess!**

N

neighborhood

A **neighborhood** is a part of a city or town. Jim walks to the store in his **neighborhood**.

P

paints

Paints are liquids with colors in them. Dip the big brushes into the **paints**.

pal

A **pal** is a friend. Benny is my best **pal**.

pants

People wear **pants** over their legs. Lucy's **pants** have two big pockets.

pet

A **pet** is an animal who lives with you. My cat Sam is the best **pet** ever!

plant
A **plant** is anything alive that is not a person or an animal. We have a **plant** with big green leaves in our kitchen.

Pop
Pop is one name for a grandfather. I call my mother's father **Pop**.

S

school
A **school** is a place where students learn from teachers. I learn to read at **school**.

storm
A **storm** is strong wind or snow. Lots of rain fell during the storm.

street
A **street** is a road in a city or a town. We live on a very busy **street**.

T

takes

The word **takes** can mean to travel by. Mia **takes** the bus to school.

this

This means something that is near you. **This** is the book I'm taking home.

train

A **train** is a group of railroad cars. This summer my family is going on a **train** ride.

W

wet

Wet means covered with liquid. Juan got **wet** when he went out in the rain.

what

The word **what** is used to ask questions. **What** did you eat for breakfast?

window

A **window** is an open place in a wall. Sasha opened the **window.**

Acknowledgments

Curious George's®Day at School, text by Houghton Mifflin Harcourt and illustrated by H.A. Rey and Margaret Rey. Text copyright © 2010 by Houghton Mifflin Harcourt Publishing Company. Illustrations copyright © 2010 by H.A. Rey and Margaret Rey. Reprinted by permission of Houghton Mifflin Harcourt Publishing Company. All rights reserved.

The character, Curious George®, including without limitation the character's name and the character's likenesses, are registered trademarks of Houghton Mifflin Harcourt Publishing Company. Curious George logo is a tradmark of Houghton Mifflin Harcourt Publishing Company. Add to front or back cover and/or spine of every book and advertisements: Curious George®

"Damon & Blue" from *My Man Blue* by Nikki Grimes. Copyright © 1999 by Nikki Grimes. Reprinted by permission of Dial Books for Young Readers, a division of Penguin Young Readers Group, a member of Penguin Group (USA) Inc., 345 Hudson Street, New York, NY 10014 and Curtis Brown, Ltd.

"Jambo" from *Nightfeathers* by Sundaira Morninghouse. Copyright © 1989 by Sundaira Morninghouse. Reprinted by permission of Open Hand Publishing, LLC (www.openhand.com).

"Wait for Me" by Sarah Wilson from *June Is a Tune That Jumps on a Stair*. Copyright © 1992 by Sarah Wilson. Reprinted by permission of the author.

Credits

Photo Credits

Placement Key: (t) top, (b) bottom, (r) right, (l) left, (bg) background, (fg) foreground, (i) inset
9 (tc) ©Image Source/Corbis; **10** (t) ©Ariel Skelley/Corbis; (b) ©Ariel Skelley/Corbis; **11** (tl) ©Bob Krist/Corbis; (tr) ©Ariel Skelley/Corbis; (bl) ©Dirk Anschutz/Stone/Getty Images; (br) ©Paul Austring Photography/First Light/Getty Images; **13** © Rommel/Masterfile; **34-35** ©Heide Benser/zefa/Corbis; **36-37** ©Colin Hogan/Alamy; **38** (tl) ©Ryan McVay/Photodisc/Alamy; (tr) ©SW Productions/Photodisc/Getty Images; (bl) ©Juniors Bildarchiv/Alamy; (br) ©Gay Bumgarner/Photographer's Choice/Getty Images; **39** (tl) ©Julian Winslow/Corbis; (cl) ©CMCD/PhotoDisc; (bl) ©Rachel Watson/Stone/Getty Images; (tr) ©Masterfile; (cr) Photospin; **42** (t) ©Amy Etra/PhotoEdit; (b) ©Spencer Grant/PhotoEdit; **43** (tl) ©Sascha Pflaeging/Riser/Getty Images; (bl) ©Richard Hutchings/PhotoEdit; (br) ©Jupiter Images/Comstock Images/Alamy; **(tr)** ©Thomas Barwick/Riser/Getty Images; **44** (b) © Masterfile; **46** ©Courtesy of Raúl Colón; **66-67** ©Douglas Keister/Corbis; **68** (bg) ©Photodisc/Don Farrall, Lightworks Studio; (tr) ©Spencer Grant/PhotoEdit; (br) ©Authors Image/Alamy; (bl) ©Matthias Engelien/Alamy; (tl) ©David Young-Wolff/PhotoEdit; **69** (b) ©Glow Images/Alamy; **70** (tl) SW Productions/PhotoDisc/GettyImages; (tr) Gay Bumgarner/Photographers Choice/GettyImages; **71** (bl) ©Patrick Bennett/Corbis; (tr) Corbis; (cr) ©Look Photography/Beateworks/Corbis; (tl) ©Dave King/Dorling Kindersley/Getty Images; (cl) PhotoObjects; **74** (t) ©Michael Newman/PhotoEdit; (b) ©Ellen